Dov

Terry Beresford

chipmunkapublishing
the mental health publisher

Terry Beresford

Published by
Chipmunkapublishing
PO Box 6872
Brentwood
Essex CM13 1ZT
United Kingdom

http://www.chipmunkapublishing.com

Chipmunkapublishing gratefully acknowledge the support of Arts Council England.

"A fireman, to be successful, must enter buildings: He must get in below, above, on every side, from opposite houses, over back walls, over side walls, through panels of doors, through windows, through loopholes cut by himself in the gates, the walls, the roof; He must know how to reach the attic from the basement by ladders placed on half-burned stairs, and the basement from the attic by rope made fast on a chimney.

His whole success depends on his getting in and remaining there and he must always carry his appliances with him, as without them he is of no use."

E. Massey Shaw

Terry Beresford

Dedicated to

Jeanne – My wife
Peg and Mick – My parents
My three children, Julie, Kevin and Steven, and my
grandchildren
Sian, Alfie and Mia for their ideas and inspiration

Also thanks to:-
Mrs. S. Chesney – Basildon Mind
Mr. C.L. Goldsmith – Basildon Mind
Mrs. P. Holdsworth – Basildon Mind
Mr. L. Beedon – Basildon Mind
Mr. P. Barry – Basildon Mind
Mr. M Stothard - British Empire Medal – ex-London
Fire Brigade
Mr. P. Slade – ex-London Fire Brigade
Mr. M. Jared – Retired
Mr. H. Wynne – Historian

Mr. H. Snelling – British Empire Medal – ex-London
Fire Brigade

& Fire-fighters everywhere

Terry Beresford

Foreword by Mr. C.L. Goldsmith
(Retired – London Fire Brigade)

My first reaction when I was asked to write this foreword was one of fear. Having given the matter much thought, I find I am enjoying it. I have known the author – Terry Beresford – for more than thirty years, and have shared some of the traumatic experiences about which he writes, and some not mentioned. There were many humorous moments that helped us to retain our sanity. He enjoyed his time in the Brigade, and has maintained a deep interest since his retirement. He is a very caring person, and keeps in contact with his many friends.

Writing this book has been a painstaking challenge for him, and has revived many happy memories, and some very sad ones.

Terry Beresford

Brief History of the London Fire Brigade

Roman Times

Fire-fighters were known as vigils and they were hand-picked. Napoleon used his best soldiers to be fire-fighters. In William the Conqueror's times, they had fire-prevention methods, although this was extremely basic.

1600 AD

This era saw the first primitive fire appliance. They were large syringes known as fire squirts, maintained at the expense of the parish. In fact, they were virtually useless.

2nd September 1666

On this date, The Great Fire of London occurred. After only five days, the city that Shakespeare had known lay in ashes. Only six people were reported to have died, although it is very likely that many more had perished. Water from rivers was used to extinguish the fires. An area of one and a half miles by half a mile was totally destroyed. 373 acres inside the city wall, 63 acres outside, 87 churches, and 13,200 houses were also destroyed by the fire. It came to a halt at Temple Church near Holborn Bridge. After the Great Fire, wooden houses were largely replaced with brick ones, and the owners were responsible for insuring their own properties. The affixing of a metal firemark to the wall would ensure your home was protected against fire. However, if a rival company came along, they would let it burn.

1833

The London Fire Engine Establishment was formed. On its formation, Mr. James Braidwood took over as Superintendent. He had 19 stations, discipline was strict and the men operated a 24-hour duty system with little leave.

1861

A riverside warehouse caught fire in Tooley Street. In the early stages of the fire, Braidwood was killed when a wall collapsed on him. Following Braidwood's death, Capt. Eyre Massey Shaw came to the fore and in 1866 the Metropolitan Fire Brigade Act was passed. Shaw expanded the use of steam fire-engines and telegraph systems. He also took over the Society for the Protection of Life from Fire in 1868. The Prince of Wales often attended fires as a fire-fighter. He was a good friend of Shaw's.

1889 – 1891

Newly-formed London County Council took over control of the Brigade from the Metropolitan Board of Works. Shaw revolted against it, as there were more rigid controls on his activities. He resigned in 1891. He was knighted by Queen Victoria on his last day of service.

1904 -1941

Motor vehicles were now used, and the last horse-drawn steamers were withdrawn in 1921. Between the wars, a new Headquarters was built at the side of the river Thames.

1939-1945

Firemen were now full-time Auxiliary Fire Service and National Fire Service, but it was not until the summer of 1940 that they saw any action – The Blitz. Winston Churchill, in one of his famous speeches, dubbed the firemen "The heroes with grimy faces".

1948-1965

Mr. F.W. Delve C.B.E. took charge of the National Fire Service in 1948. He reshaped the Brigade, worn out appliances and equipment would go, and accommodation and training facilities would be improved.

1962

Delve was knighted and after his retirement, he was succeeded by his deputy Mr. L.W.T. Leete, who was the first man to rise through the ranks to become Chief Officer.
1963

The Local Government Act was passed, which

established the Greater London Council as the Fire Authority over areas previously covered by London, Middlesex, West Ham, parts of Essex, Hertfordshire, Surrey and Kent.

1966

The Queen's Review was held at Lambeth Headquarters, celebrating 100 years of Fire Service in London. The next two decades saw a number of changes. Wheeled escapes which were introduced to rescue people trapped in Victorian tenements, were replaced with lighter manoeuvrable alloy ladders, and hydraulic platforms now aid aerial fire-fighting.

1978

The National Fire Brigade strike occurred. The strike was nationwide and saw the Army drafted in to operate appliances known as "Green Goddesses", which were left over from the Auxiliary Fire Service days. When it was finally settled, a nationally agreed pay formula was in place that still survives today.

31st March 1986

A major fire at Hampton Court Palace marked the last day of the Greater London Council's existence. Control of the Fire Brigade was passed to a new body, The London Fire and Civil Defence Authority (LFCDA); which is comprised of a panel of councillors, one from each of London's thirty-two boroughs plus a representative from the City of London. The late 1980s saw a number of tragedies befall London.

1987

Thirty-one people died, including a fire officer, as a result of a fire in King's Cross underground station.

1988

Thirty-five people died after two trains collided in South London.

1989

Fifty-one people perished when a pleasure cruiser, The Marchioness, struck a barge and sunk on the Thames.

The resources of the London Fire Brigade were tested on these occasions, but the expertise and professionalism of the fire-fighters saw them through.

Chapter One

Through the Arch
Dedicated to my family

The end – the end of the line. Fenchurch Street Railway Station, London. E.C.1. I'm nearly there. My heart thumped. "Could I do this which is asked of me?" I thought. A short walk to Tower Hill underground station. Ten minutes later, my final stop. Borough, South-East London. Into the lift and out onto the street. It was quite dark, November you see. Following remembered directions from my interview, I progressed along Lant Street, another of Dickens' abodes, he certainly got around. Turning right into Southwark Bridge Road, I neared my destiny. Pass or fail, I will have tried and kept my word to the man who had trusted me in this career – his career.

"I won't let you down" I said, and wouldn't, as this book will tell. The man's name? Albert Smith – Station Officer, London Fire Brigade, my best friend Terry's father. A rough diamond, but a man I had respected since I was a lad of around 13 years old. He recommended me for this career, knowing that I had had many jobs since leaving school. I was only 19 and I was going into a real man's job. My uncle – Stan Hooks, British Empire Medal, served for 30 years and on his retirement was the Fire Service National Benevolent Fund Secretary for the Eastern Command area of the London Fire Brigade. As a child he was my hero, my favourite uncle. Now I've given you a clue to my goal – a career as a London Fireman.

I crossed the main road and could now see a large archway – the entrance to the London Fire Brigade Training Centre. Training goes back to the nineteenth century here, when Eyre Massey Shaw was the Chief Fire Officer of the Metropolitan Fire Brigade in 1866 – its formation. Prior to this, it was the London Fire Engine Establishment and the Chief Fire Officer was James Braidwood, from the City of Edinburgh Fire Service. Massey Shaw was a good friend of Edward – Prince Regent – Queen Victoria's son. He attended and fought many fires alongside the firemen, who were mainly recruited from naval seamen.

Me? No such background, but I was here now. I slipped a little as I entered the cobble-stoned yard through the arch. Perhaps I was distracted by the 70-foot drill tower immediately in front of me. A modern, grey monolithic structure of seven floors, out of place here, I thought. The surrounding buildings and the other tower were much older. The buildings consisted of four floors and a basement and were Victorian. It was as if I'd gone back in time. My thoughts were interrupted by a voice.
"Good morning lad. New recruit?"
"Y-yes" I said nervously. "Fireman Beresford, reporting for duty sir".
"Well done. Follow me" he said. His name was Station Officer Swanton, and he was the Administrative Officer at the centre. I noticed his

fingers – they were bent inwards. He suffered with arthritis – a very common condition in firemen even now. He asked me into the office, and put the kettle on.

"Come far?" he asked.

"Rainham, Essex, sir". I thought how nice he seemed, not like how I imagined. There weren't many like him, and it didn't take long to find out. A knock at the office door, a polite "Come in" from the Station Officer, and a lad entered and said "'Ello boss – I'm 'ere".

"Well done," said Station Officer Swanton "but what is your name?"

"Sorry mate. Evans – Graham Evans. Alwight?" The Station Officer shook his head and smiled. I was later to find out that Station Officer "Charlie" Swanton was nearing retirement and had served for many years at the Southwark Station, which was one of the busiest in London.

"Sit down Mr. Evans. Station Officer Clark won't be long. He's your instructor for the next sixteen weeks. Call him 'Sir' lad, or else", he quipped. It was now 8.45am and the room had swelled with bodies somewhat since I'd arrived. No one spoke, just waited. Not for long. A man in uniform entered the room. All of 6 foot, in a cap depicting a Guardsman's peak over his eyes. This was Station Officer Clark. He was notorious as an instructor, and gave little quarter.

"Do it, or you're out" he often said. This man proved to be a total bastard, and I believe he'd never had a recruit failure, and was proud of that.

"Good morning lads" he said. He then introduced himself.

Chapter Two

The First Heat

"Station Officer Clark is my name. You are nobodies at the moment ladees! I will be your instructor for the next sixteen weeks, and when you leave you will be highly trained and ready for your career in the London Fire Brigade. This is the finest training centre in the country. They come from all over to train here." I was stunned by this guy – he was awesome, like a robot. He marched smartly to the desk where Station Officer Swanton was sitting.

"Morning Charlie. How's the family?" he said.

"Grandchildren have colds, Jim". He replied. "Let's have the list of names of this mob, before I get angry and upset 'em all". He's already scared the shit out of us all, by Christ.

"Let's have a butchers" he continued. "Good heavens, Evans! Is yer dad in the job, lad?"

"No sir" replied Evans. "Dad's a doctor Mat – sir" he corrected himself remembering Mr. Swanton's advice.

"Well ladee, you may need one when you're done here. I hope you're all fit, because you'll have to be". He looked around the room glaring – "You look like a bunch of yobs – get yer 'aircut – now, and I mean now. Go!" Off we went, all twelve of us to find a local barber. Some had no money, some lent and some borrowed – team spirit had started.

On our return – all shorn – he inspected us. Three went back for more off. I was O.K. I had had a short time in the army cadets and knew what was required. It was now 10.15a.m. and parades had finished and drills were starting in the yard.

"Come on ladees" roared Clark. "Let's have a look at some ladder drill – hook ladders to start I feel." I had seen Station Officer Clark in action on my interview day, as he gently guided his last squad into shape for their pass out parade. Soft and gentle he spoke, so I knew he was O.K. at least, not that he showed it much. He was a mercenary, no quarter during training. At lectures, he mellowed but never dropped his guard until the end of training where he proved a very nice chap indeed, first class he was, but pure hell under his instructions. He was the ultimate bastard, believe me – just my luck!

We shuffled into the yard through the arch once again, and entered into the drill yard. Clark gave us a lecture in the freezing cold. We all had a short length of rope to practice knots and lines with. As the instructor asked one person a question, he got another to tie a knot. We watched in awe as the ladder drills developed. Four squads were in action, two doing hook ladders, another carry-downs, the last pump drill. The hook ladder was climbed vertically. It was 14 foot long and incorporated a toothed-bill that, when in use, the hook was at right angles to the ladder itself. When not in use, the bill folded into a section of the ladder, and was secured to the main ladder via a spring bolt. It was used where no normal ladder could go, tight alleys or passageways, narrow windowsills, even from the top of conventional ladders, including turntables at 100 foot. It would hook onto a windowsill and the toothed bill would bite into the sill. One or two men would scale the building on this ladder by carrying and hooking on the ladder to each floor as they went. You could go as high as you liked.

Suddenly Clark went ballistic. I thought the young lad he'd picked on – one of the youngest – Thomas – was going to cry or run out. Clark came back as though nothing had happened, and showed him the knot again. Thomas did it well and to Clark's satisfaction.

"Well done ladee" he said. He went round the whole squad of twelve without a problem. A.D.O. Hunter, who ran or ruled the training centre, marched across to Station Officer Clark, whispered in his ear and Clark went off. Hunter's reputation was as good as Clark's. He taught us the proper way to salute – up, down, up, down till Clark came back some minutes later. He thanked Mr. Hunter and joined our ranks again. We could just see some of the drills going on at the nearby tower. We were shown a self-rescue knot – well I'm glad we didn't have to use it - all ours fell apart. Clark for a change just laughed and took the piss. He put us in line and taught us more marching. He yelled and yelled to his heart's content, to see how far we would go.

We halted near the drill towers. One squad was doing a two-man drill with a large pack on their backs. This held a line or rope inside and was quite heavy. One man wore a hooked belt, and when hooked at the head of the first ladder, his partner would punch the other ladder up to him. He would grab it and push the hook ladder to the next floor. Both would climb and repeat the action until the seventh floor of the training tower, and then they would change their belt over to the other man and proceed to climb down. This was the ultimate ladder drill, believe me, and you had to do it to pass the course. One-man hook ladders were in use on the other side of the tower. The drill meant the man would sit in on each sill and punch the ladder up himself, until he reached the designated level. Carry-down drills were also going on, and the trainees were carrying each other down the wheeled escape ladder from the third floor of the old wooden tower at the bottom of the training school yard. No safety lines were in use at this time as I remember, so you really had to rely and trust your partner.

Finally, the pump drill was a case of getting a large charged length of hose to the second floor via an extension ladder, then man-handling it to the fifth floor via the integral 'Jacob's Ladder' then down again, the hose fully charged all the time. That was hard work as we were to find out very soon.
"Come on lads" roared Clark, "Lecture room 4, first floor, opposite the old tower in ten minutes O.K.?!" We snapped out of our mesmerised state from watching the action, and hastily went to find the next venue.

Clark was waiting for us. He had sat down with his hat and coat removed, reading our names list. He looked different. He was balding, and his red hair slightly grey. He was around the forties mark, but looked younger. He certainly looked very fit and carried not an ounce of fat on him. We settled down at our desks and he called out our names, followed by him telling us that after lunch we would be leaving by personnel carrier to Tottenham Hale for our kit, etc. Our course duration was sixteen weeks, others only twelve. One of our group, Meeks, asked the instructor why we had to do the longer course.

"Cos you're bloody thick" was his blunt reply. We asked no more, remaining quiet listening to Clark informing us of his career in the Guards and the London Fire Brigade over the past twenty years or so. It made interesting listening and made us all think, especially his work experiences at the front line of fire-fighting; he was mainly relating nasty incidents, possibly to see our reaction to his harrowing saga.

"Break for lunch ladees" he said, checking his watch.

"Be back in the reception office at 1:30p.m. sharp. We will not wait for anyone. Right, downstairs and line up". We had to march everywhere, even to lunch breaks, although I must say, our first spot of 'marching' had to be seen to be believed. He left us at the steps of the canteen, which was on the first floor of this vast Victorian complex. Many of us had no money, so again we begged and borrowed between ourselves. For myself, I had enough for a cheese roll and a cuppa, my return train ticket already paid for the journey home at 5.30p.m.

After lunch, we sauntered over to the office in ones and twos. Little did we know Clark saw all this from his room three floors up, and was not happy. The whole squad waited in the reception, and soon after Clark drew up in a dark green personnel carrier for our journey.

"All out" he screamed through the door. "Line up in file alongside the wall". He gave us hell and marched us up and down that yard for an hour before we left to get our kit. What a sight. Remember, we were all in various civvy outfits, and many had never marched before. We pulled out of the training centre yard, albeit an hour late, heading for our destination.

Kitted out, we returned in darkness around 5 o'clock. Keys and lockers were allocated, and we shoved our gear in the lockers and left for home. Mixed feelings for me on my first day; although I had enjoyed it, but could I do all that would be asked of me? My confidence waned. Having told my parents of my day, hook ladders and all, I went to bed only to be firmly informed by my dad the next morning,

"Don't tell your mum anything more about those ladders". She hadn't slept all night for worrying. I had to keep it to myself, not too bad though, as I could always tell my girlfriend Jeanne of my escapades. Although, sometime later I was jolted into silence again even from her, following a tragedy some short time into my career.

The following day held many surprises. Our instructor inspected our lockers immediately after roll call, and tore every one of us to pieces, except one chap – Mac Butler, an ex-soldier – a sergeant I believe. He had folded everything into his locker in a fashion satisfactory to Clark. But for the remainder, we spent an hour sorting our gear from off the floor and placing it neatly in our lockers, as it was to stay. We were then informed that we had been 'selected' to form part of the display for H.M. Queen Elizabeth II Centenary Review at Lambeth H.Q. We were issued with brass helmets and Victorian tunics for the event, although we didn't need them as my squad got the job of clearing up the horse's mess as the Victorian pageant was carried out, much to our dismay.

Unfortunately, when the day of the pageant came, I had developed severe blisters and infection on both my heels. My new shoes had taken their toll and I was unable to perform my duties for around a fortnight, lectures only, and of course I watched all the drills. Clark gave them hell, but I still relished the idea of getting back to full training duties. I did, but not under Station Officer Clark, who felt he may get me to the standard required with the physical side – drills, etc., but the theory side would be difficult as I had missed more lessons due to my having treatment s. I was back-squadded by two weeks, joining Station Officer Ron Perrott's squad on the following Monday. They had only started on the previous week, and I slotted into the timetable nicely. Station Officer Perrott, an uncle to us all, a chubby man with a sense of humour and not as fierce as his predecessor, except when upset by our shortfalls in training. We did the lot, initial hose drills, carry downs, hook ladders, lectures etc., maths even – hence the sixteen week course!

My new instructor was a warm family man who guided us rather than bullied us, as my friend 'Mac Butler' informed me Clark did all the time – no political correctness around then, or ethnic minorities or women in training either, not in the London Fire Brigade anyhow. Many outside brigades attended here and once trained, you could go confidently to your station, that's for sure; training was that good. Our instructor also hadn't had a recruit fail the course, some left of course, and others proved not suitable, usually within the first few weeks of training. Training was hard; the theory work alone was a mountain of notes upon notes, no time for socialising at all. I saw Jeanne once at weekends throughout training. The practical side was hard but enjoyable. I had little fear of ladders etc., although strangely I 'froze' whilst changing from one hook ladder to another during drills, and was informed if I couldn't do it, I was out. I did it the next day, and all was forgotten. I'll never know why that happened. It was just the once.

Mac Butler's squad had passed out two weeks before us, and Mac was not up to scratch on his theory and was looking to be back-squadded to our squad. He was shattered, until he heard he had passed as Station Officer Clark had spoken to the centre Commander saying he would trust Mac in any crisis situation whatsoever, surely saving Mac's career, as I'm sure he would have left that day. The work got no easier, the paperwork and notes piled high. Many struggled, especially on practical work. I was average all round, so I was told. During my time here, I learnt a lot about team work, relying on others, and overcoming fears. Ron Perrott was great at spotting the warning signs and would act accordingly to be harder or softer on us. Mostly, he would be, let's say – firm, with us. Many of the other instructors were bastards too; however, you often saw their better side, especially at pass out day.

During our time here, we had climbed seven floors with a portable ladder and a line carrier and down again, got soaked to the skin hundreds of times, fell over thousands of times, carried down a ladder, a person, been carried down on a man's back, joined ladders together at a height of 60 foot, sat for hours and hours at home and at the training centre studying, had umpteen bollockings, and had three showers a day. We must be mad; well you had to be to do this job. We only had two weeks to go. Time to clean up the centre, lockers washed out, gear tidy and clean. Our uniform was immaculate, ready for pass out parade on the Monday week. A.D.O. Hunter took that parade and did the inspection, most were in order. Our time had come – finals week, pass out. I passed the theory examinations, first aid, maths and so on. They were held on the Monday and Tuesday. Practicals and final interviews took place on the Wednesday and Thursday at Headquarters Lambeth.

All went well, we all passed, ten of us. We lost two

during training, one was injured and back squadded, and another left of his own accord a week into training. So Ron Perrott was happy, especially as we had arranged a night out in the West End and presented him with a briefcase for putting up with us all for 16 weeks. He too came back into my career in the late '70's as my Divisional Officer. He remained the same, a true gentleman.

Our stations had been allocated a week before. Mine was F27 Bow Red Watch. Our final interview preceded our leaving on the Friday afternoon. Transport had been arranged to take us to our new stations. At 1 o'clock we drove out through the arch.

I'd done it. I reminisced over my training. The hook ladder drills, escape ladder drills, down in the breathing apparatus room, Station Officer Clark, Station Officer Perrott and one other, Station Officer Ben Gunn, who, whilst Station Officer Perrott was off sick, we were allocated Station Officer Ben Gunn. He made us do the ultimate on the hook ladder, two ladders, two men and a line and carrier on one person's back. Not only did he make us do a two-man drill, but a one-man drill too. Some went up four times – good job it wasn't windy – it was for some, I tell you. Ben gave us escape ladder drills and carry-downs, until we could do it in our sleep. He dished out more notes, but we had no time to read them though. One from our group, Greenhall, complained and was told to read on the train home and in bed. Luckily for us, Station Officer Perrott came back after three days. He heard what we had been up to, so he too went through all drills again, to make sure we were up to scratch. We must have been, because the next two days were spent on catching up with our studies. It was now time to leave for our allocated fire stations, as real firemen, albeit probationary. When my friend Terry went in to the Fire Service, my thoughts were 'I couldn't do that'. Why did I think that? Lack of confidence; my downfall throughout. Terry's dad Albert came to mind. He trusted and recommended me, now I'd been there, done it and got the T shirt even. Training was hard, no London recruit would deny that, as I said Southwark is awesome, a fine training centre, like training in Victorian times. Amazing.

The van stopped.
"Holloway – Fireman Tarbun" called the driver. Tom Tarbun was one of our best recruits and the station he had been allocated was one of the busiest in London, if not the country. We helped him with his kit and shook hands. As we drove off, Tom just stood there, as if in a daze. I think we must have all felt a bit like that. 'Stoney' Edwards was next, Shoreditch. C. Division Headquarters, a very large and busy station. 'Stoney' opened up the back of the van, said goodbye and disappeared into the station.
"Last stop F27 Bow lad" said the driver. He was from F30 Leytonstone and knew all the men at Bow.
"You'll be alright there lad, a damn good old fashioned watch, plus a good bunch of Officers". I felt relaxed thinking of our training days.

Chapter Three

The Heat is on

Dedicated to the memory of those who died at Dudgeon's Wharf 17th July 1969

I arrived at F27 Bow in the early afternoon, having dropped off two of my training school colleagues. The van entered the back yard. I was informed by the driver that my watch – Red – were on duty today. It seemed most of them were in the yard scrubbing off the fire hose, prior to hanging it to dry up the 50 foot tower, very similar to those at training school. I had visited the station the week previous, and 'Mac' Butler was on duty with the blue watch, hardly had time for a chat as they had two calls during my visit. The second 'shout' left me alone in the station, and after a short wait, I decided to go home, prior to their return.

The driver now helped me into the locker room with my kit, and was chatting to the men in the yard. As I stood waiting, the doors opened and a fireman appeared.
"Hello mate. Georgie Potts – Pottsy to you. What's your name?"
"Terry" I said. George was a short man around 5'7" and had served nearly thirty years, coming through the blitz in London. Two others came in and George disappeared, only to return shortly with my locker keys.
"Hello there" said one, "I am Len Haines and this is Jim Lamble, the mess manager". I introduced

29

myself again as another man came in, a leading fireman from his rank markings.

"Ron Randall" he said shaking my hand. "Pleased to meet you. What did you do before joining the job, Terry?"

"Building work, labouring, roofing, that kinda stuff" I said.

"Well, that's handy Ron", uttered Jim. "I think you've a part-time job Terry. Not bad eh! Only been in the station five minutes".

True enough, I did get a part-time job with Ron who was doing up his house in his off-duty time. I helped him for about a year. I felt at home; they made me feel welcome. Most of the watch were older men. One, Fred Smythe was a hurricane fighter pilot. John Bennett, who I was yet to meet, was a despatch rider during the war. Dave Harris and Lionel Brunsden were working in the yard. These were the babies of the watch. Dave was a month or so in front of me and Lionel six months. Ron took me outside to meet them. Dave was my age, and Lionel was much older. Station Officer Griffiths and Sub Officer Meeson were in the station office upstairs. I went to meet them, having a stand-easy with the watch, and then left at 6pm with Dave as he lived near me, for our journey home.

I was due back on my first of two day shifts on Wednesday. I looked forward to a four day break with no notes to study even more so. Dave and I met up at the railway station as agreed at 7:30am. He told me about the station and some of the jobs he'd attended in his short time on Red Watch. I relished my future with a little apprehension. The first day was uneventful, no shouts, station work, drills and a lecture as I recall took place. Having met all the men on the watch now, I really felt at home, albeit a little nervous.

My first shout was the following day; a derelict shop alight on F28 Homerton's ground. What a strange feeling, that first time, going into the unknown. I had experienced nothing like this. Fred was driving the pump escape and called to me.
"Stick with the Leading Fireman Terry, he's riding the back of the pump. He'll look out for you as we arrive". He did too, grabbing me, and we kicked the doors in to gain entry to this shop which was well alight. We entered with a large line of charged hose. It was great! A large crowd had gathered as the blaze was quite spectacular, not as frightening inside as you may think, although dense smoke drifted across the road and flames roared from the first floor windows. After twenty minutes, we were on our way. Homerton's crew remained at the scene damping down. I felt we'd done a good job; I'd had my 'baptism of fire'.

My first watchroom duty was a week or two later. I had been under instructions up until then; filling in log books, preparing appliance rider boards, answering fire and phone calls. It was around 8.50am. I had taken over from the White Watch duty man. I booked on and waited, nervously going through all I had to do. I stood by the watchroom door looking across the appliance room of this 1910 built fire station, originally built to accommodate horse-drawn steam fire engines. Our locker room was in fact meant to have been the stables, although the horses never came. Mechanical-drawn appliances were used when the station was finished. The floor was grooved to allow drainage from the horses to pass outside at the front of the station. My daydream was shattered at around 9am. The teleprinter bell sounded, followed by the fire call bell. This was the time for the call bell to be tested, and everyone presumed I had forgotten to sound the three short rings prior to the test at every change of watch. This was, however, a real call. It took a while for the crew to realise and this caused a slight delay. The printer tapped out 'House fire – Coborn Road Bow E3' followed by the route card index number. With all the information in my hand, I jumped aboard and we were on our way.

Coborn Road was only minutes away. It was actually on F24 Burdett Road's ground, although, it was easier for us to get there as F24 was on the other side of the increasingly busy Mile End Road. We arrived first, confronted by thick smoke billowing from the basement of a terraced Victorian four-storey house. Station Officer Goldsmith followed with his crew from F24. He immediately sent a priority assistance message, 'make pumps four – persons reported'. I assisted in attacking the fire through the basement window with a hose jet. Crews were rigging in breathing apparatus to enable them to search the flat from the rear. We could see nothing through the thick acrid smoke at this time. We shut our jet down to enable the crews to search inside. The smoke cleared and we saw on a bed, what appeared to be the remains of a clothing shop dress model, soon realising it was the charred remains of an elderly lady; her midriff was burnt through with her upper and lower parts still intact. Our jet was not required further and Station Officer Griffiths called for a crew to assist in cutting away and damping down, prior to the arrival of a doctor to inspect the body before removal to the mortuary. I was now in the basement standing over the remains. The single bed was in ashes, probably smouldered all night. The sight was unreal. I had had my first fatal fire, commonly known as a 'stiff', within weeks of joining the front line of the fire service.

My return to the station was greeted with Lionel opening the doors to allow the appliance's entry. He had been out on duty for a time at F26 Bethnal Green, and had now returned, missing out on this one. He'd been at Bow for 5 or 6 months, and had yet to be involved with a fatal fire.

"What a start" he quipped. I felt we'd done our best. The lady was way beyond help hours before we arrived. A week later, we attended a fire in a fourth floor flat on F28's ground. We arrived a little after C23 Stoke Newington's crew with Station Officer 'Blood' Jones in charge. Our entry revealed the body of a woman lying over a radiant two-bar room heater in much the same state as my previous 'stiff' – two in less than a month. Once again on our return, Lionel, who was on the pump escape and did not attend this call, said, "Cor blimey Terry, you must be a jinx. You've not been here five minutes and we ain't stopped". He'd not have to wait long though for his 'first', for only days later we went to a building site in Roman Road. A labourer had called the Brigade, as his bricklayer working on the third floor had collapsed. On climbing the scaffolding we discovered the man lying dead. It was later established he'd had a heart attack. We lowered the body to the ground for removal. "Bloody jinx" Lionel said once again. Perhaps I was. The station had been a lot busier than normal. This included a six-pump fire on a rubber dump not far from the station. Bow had around 100 calls a month, compared with surrounding stations, which were up in the 200s at times.

I was enjoying the job, unaffected by my first few weeks on the front line. My older colleagues were very supportive to Lionel, Dave and myself. We would remain lifelong family friends, such was the bond with the job. Socially, myself and Jeanne would join the watch at various occasions, weddings, retirements etc. although one sad occasion was attended by myself and a couple of others from Bow, to the funeral of two firemen who had been killed whilst fire-fighting in West London, their deaths being caused by the explosion of a gas cylinder on a building site.

I had attended many fires in my first year, large and small. One attended was Dudgeon's Wharf, on 4th July 1969. Len Haines had been listening to the Brigade radio network and heard F23 Millwall ask for assistance at Dudgeon's Wharf. Eight pumps and two turntable ladders were required. Len immediately informed everyone to be prepared to 'go on', which we did. On arrival we saw a storage tank, its roof off, with flames 50 feet into the air. We climbed to the top of an adjacent tank and poured foam and water on to and into the blazing tank. It took around two hours to bring it under control. That evening I told Jeanne about it. I was on annual leave for the next two weeks, and one day when Jeanne arrived home she was in tears. "Five firemen have been killed at that Dudgeon's Wharf" she said, showing me the newspaper headlines. I had heard nothing on the news, having been in the garden all day. I phoned the station and spoke to Leading Fireman Roy Cox, who gave me the names of those killed. All blue watch and fire-fighters from the F22 and F23 stations. I never spoke to my girlfriend about my job after this, it would worry her. The tragedy occurred at 11.22am on 17th July 1969, the initial attendance being F23's pump escape and pump, F22's pump and a foam tender from L21 East Ham. Initially, the fire was deemed out on arrival. The firemen were directed to tank 97. Two workmen were holding a branch on top of the tank. They informed the Station Officer that it had been put out, and there were no signs to dispute this. Several firemen climbed the tank joining one of the workmen to inspect, and to apply a cooling jet inside the tank. What the fire brigade were not told was that 20 foot flames were issuing from the tank some ten minutes earlier before the firemen arrived. Ground crews were opening a cover on the side of the tank to see inside when the tank roof was blown off, hurling the six unfortunate men who were still upon it high into the air, and landing around the quayside or into 5 foot deep oil sludge. One, Fireman Appleby F22, fell back into tank 97, the tank top being blown 125 feet away on to the top of tank 4. It was folded in half. Two men, Station Officer Snelling and Fireman Richman gallantly entered tank 97 from the now roofless top, descending by way of the inside ladder, and although they found Fireman Appleby, he was beyond human aid. Station Officer Snelling and Fireman Richman were later awarded the B.E.M. from Her Majesty the Queen. Those who died were Sub Officer Michael Gamble, Fireman Trevor Carvosso, Fireman Alfred Smee, Fireman John Appleby, and Fireman Terence Breen. A civilian contractor Mr. Reginald Adams also died.

Far-reaching safety regulations including Hazchem were instigated following this tragedy, possibly leading to the fine health and safety at work regulations in force today. Station Officer Griffiths had left prior to the Dudgeon's tragedy, and dear old Pottsy had retired. He unfortunately passed away in the early 1970's. Station Officer Goldsmith was now in charge. He and Ray Dean had joined us from the now closed Burdett Road Station. I was at training school with Ray. He was a great guy, having served in the Royal Medical Corps prior to joining the London Fire Brigade. We became known as the 'terrible twins' on the watch, as we always seemed to be in the thick of it on fires. Lionel was still with us and was now driving the appliances. Dave had been transferred to the white watch, and Jim had retired. I took over his duties as mess manager for the red watch, a task I did for three years. My father had a butcher's shop, so I was able to get the day to day meals easily.

Having attended so many incidents, rather too many to recall, some do come to mind, for instance the man trapped down a mud-filled excavation who we rescued safely. The sad aftermath when a person or persons jump to their death after being trapped in a fire, the humans rescued and the many animals safely retrieved from incidents. Other watches too had their tales to tell. Two men on the white watch received awards for their rescue of a man from a rooftop during a fire. A baby, in a pram flattened by an overturned container lorry, safely retrieved. Road traffic accidents were numerous; we all had those, countless unnecessary as many of the cases being caused by drink driving.

One nasty job I didn't attend, it was the blue watch that did, was where a sack lift was being used at a factory by two men to gain access to floors whilst working. The lift collapsed whilst moving and dragged the two men with it. The shaft ran with blood and the bodies were trapped between the lift shaft and the lift itself on an upper floor. Both bodies had to be extricated by the Brigade. We retrieved bodies from the nearby canal and lock at Bow, not a nice thing handling dead bodies, although in the main we were successful in our rescue attempts, thank God. My watch attended a fatal accident involving a double-decker bus. A small child had fallen under the wheels whilst the vehicle was moving; becoming trapped by the hair tangled around the prop-shaft and dragged some distance. The worst jobs were those involving children. Even at this early stage of my career I had seen some heroics, even been involved in them myself, it never occurs to you, a job has to be done.

The guys on the watch all helped each other out; be it moving house, a little electrical or plumbing work, or a lift to work even, you only had to ask. I now had a small 50cc Honda moped to get me back and forth, and at home we were involved in decorating. It was now the early 1970's, and I was involving myself in the Fire Service Benevolent Fund and a little Union work at the station. I continued to do part-time jobs here and there. I had made lifelong friends here at Bow with more to come.

March 1971 saw me suffer a double hernia operation, causing me to be off work for several weeks. My uncle Stan Hooks B.E.M arranged for Jeanne and myself to stay for a week at the Benevolent Fund's Convalescent Centre at Littlehampton. Our convalescent break was great. One week in a one-bedroom flat near the seafront for the use of fire-fighters everywhere. Today, the Fire Service Benevolent Fund has three centres; Marine Court Littlehampton, Harcombe House in Devon and the large therapy unit in Penrith – Jubilee House. I doubt you would find a better Benevolent Fund.

Whilst I was still off sick, a chance came for me to

transfer to another station, F29 Leyton, a very quiet one appliance station. A change is as good as a rest, so I took the opportunity. I was still in some pain from my operation, due to that I was unable to ride my moped, which was replaced by an old Ford Consul 1960's period. No more riding my bike in the rain and cold winds, the car was now my pride and joy.

Chapter Four

Empty Handed

I was signed off by my doctor, and returned to work having been transferred to F29 Leyton Red Watch. Hardly having time to unpack my kit and put it in my locker, I was informed that I would be on light duties for a period prior to seeing the Brigade Medical Officer and transferred temporarily to F Division Headquarters Staff, the new station at F22 Poplar. Ron Randall was now promoted and was Sub Officer in charge of this department, so I didn't mind. I did general filing duties, took phone calls, everything in fact except attend fire calls, which I missed. This work was an experience that stood me in good stead when the time came, and I was promoted. I finally arrived at Leyton proper in August. I had served approximately four and a half years at this time. I had gained qualifications in breathing apparatus and radio telephone operator. This wasn't to be enough as I soon found out from my new governor, Sub Officer Jim Docherty B.E.M. His reputation went before him. However, I was still in for a shock, albeit it proved to be the making of me. Jim was most certainly the finest Sub Officer I had the pleasure to serve with throughout my career. His reputation was as a 'bastard' of the nicest possible kind of course. He expected me to leave Leyton with many more qualifications than I had, and told me so.

"You'll have time here to concentrate on them and also get some office work under your belt, because I can do without you when I'm busy". His favourite quote, not meant personally of course, he said it to one and all. He would sit in his office and behind him was his citation, which led to him being presented his B.E.M. This was for his actions at a serious fire where he, without doubt, saved several people from a house blaze. He was himself removed to hospital following the rescues. His whole crew was commended by the Chief Officer for their actions.

It was different at Leyton; 'Jim's kingdom' drills were done en bloc, once a fortnight, the rest of the time we kept the station clean, and I mean clean. Also, we had to wear a collar and tie for meals. Many standbys from other stations tried it on with Jim, arriving improperly dressed and refusing some cleaning duties, which were now done by contractors. He would send you back to your own station if he was not satisfied, and the now defunct appliance room scrub out became a foam drill for standbys who objected. He was a law unto himself, although a gentleman and a genuine family man. We did many odd jobs at Leyton. Our regulation single fridge grew to three in number. Antiquated fittings around the station were replaced by more modern fixtures. Unwanted structures including an old fireplace disappeared within days, much to the dilemma of other watch Sub Officers. We decorated the place. Standbys would be allowed to stand down once completing a painting job. We built a shed using timber from various building sites. It was hidden at the side of the station with a salvage sheet over it whilst being built. No one ever saw it until it was finished.

The worst that one could do was to let him or the watch down, then you were in trouble. He requested you to inform him of any problems at home as he would do all in his power to assist you. The Red Watch here consisted of Leading Fireman Joe Mercer, an ex-Essex man, who served over thirty years as a Leading Fireman alone, he backed Jim to the hilt. Stan Hooper, Barry Carter, Frank Lynch the mess manager, and myself, who still provided meat from my father's shop for the mess. The station had around 60 to 70 calls a month, no standby out duties at other stations and we rarely went off our own ground. I cannot remember any large fires of any significance in my time there, but we were all very much occupied in the station.

I passed my Leading Fireman's written examination in January 1972, H.G.V. Driving Course in May 1972 and finally qualified as a turntable ladder driver in July l972, all under the Sub Officer's gentle guidance. Joe Mercer came up for retirement and we organised his do at the recently finished bar and social club at F Division Headquarters. The then Chief Officer, Joe Milner, came which was a rare occurrence. The F Divisional Commander presented Joe with his many gifts from colleagues around the Division. This was the first retirement party held at the F Division club, around 100 people attended as Joe was a very popular figure within the F Division.

In 1972, I failed my practical Leading Fireman's Exam, however the Sub had me acting-up at F30 Leytonstone, even though my colleague Barry had passed the exam. I am sure Jim did it to boost my moral. I stayed at Leytonstone for a month as Leading Fireman, and thoroughly enjoyed it. On my return, Jim continued to mould us youngsters for our day of departure. He would decide when. In September 1972, my pregnant wife called the station whilst I was on nights to say that the baby's arrival was imminent. I informed Jim, and he arranged for me to go home and see my daughter Julie Anne being born. On my return, I attended a Fire Prevention Course and qualified for it. That was enough for Jim, time they moved on. Both Barry and I were in the frame. He went first. I was to be next. He had me in the office. "Where do you want to go old Beresford?" he said.

"Euston" I replied. A busy station in the A Division. "So be it" he said. I thought he was joking, being quite happy at 29. I knew I would have to move on one day. The next shift saw me posted to A23 Euston red watch. I was stunned and I objected, having rashly mentioned Euston. I really wished to remain in the F Division – my Division. The Assistant Divisional Officer was summoned, and I asked to see the Commander. I had to leave Leyton as a new recruit had been posted in to replace me. I remained at the station until a meeting was arranged between the Divisional Commander, Sub Officer Docherty and myself. I pleaded in there to stay in the division and was successful, albeit I got a hell of a bollocking for messing them about. My posting was to be arranged, possibly F25 Shadwell, near to the Tower of London. This wasn't to be. The Fire Brigades Union became involved and I was asked if I would go to F22 Poplar Blue Watch as turntable ladder driver and mess manager. To decline would have left me up to my arse in alligators. I accepted, and on 21st January 1973 I was posted.

A better fireman now, I felt for my time with Sub Officer Docherty, who if nothing else taught me another of his favourite quotes 'Never ever go in or out of a building empty-handed, be it an extinguisher, hose line axe; always bring something out with you'. That advice still sticks in my mind to this day. If I go upstairs at home I will take an item of clothing, ironing etc. and duly bring down perhaps the dirty washing from the basket upstairs. His words are engraved on my mind – strange isn't it? Jim Docherty was perfect for me at the time, he rounded my edges off. Although, he spoke to one and all quite gruffly, we all knew it was a game to him. We had fewer calls here than at Poplar, who were very busy. I looked forward to my joining Blue Watch at Poplar, as I packed my bags for my transfer. Jim had his new recruits, and I went to bid him farewell. He shook my hand warmly and said in a broad Scottish accent, "Remember Beresford, I can do without you when I am busy". I headed off with his comments ringing in my ears.

Chapter Five

Catch 22

Well another move, another locker. Different ball game here at F22 Headquarters of the Division, with Senior Officer's accommodation and Headquarters' offices adjacent to the station. Extremely busy both day and night, three front line appliances; pump escape, pump and turntable ladder, plus a small control unit, three vans and three officers' cars all ready to go. The dustmen's strike saw 365 calls in four days, as many as the quietest London station, Biggin Hill had in a year. 700 to 800 calls were received a month during those strikes, all rubbish, and still we had the other jobs coming in. I arrived early to note that I was down to drive the turntable ladder, having never driven one to an incident. I was apprehensive about it. My new governor came into the watch room and I introduced myself. He was Station Officer Harold 'Snudge' Snelling B.E.M. gaining his award for gallantry at Dudgeon's Wharf. He was a true character, a very funny man, however he never missed any goings on at his station; you couldn't get away with much. He apologised to me for putting me on the turntable ladder on my first day, and asked if I would like to take it out for a spin. I declined, but regretted it later in the day.

Considering all that my new Station Officer had been through, he seemed so laid back and very approachable with any problems one might have. I met the watch, Tony Moon and Ray Sherman I already knew. We then had our usual cuppa to start the day. It was a Sunday as I remember. The station was vast, three floors and a sliding pole from the top of the building to the appliance room, around a 35 to 40 foot drop, four appliance bays, large mess rooms, plus officers and men's accommodation. This did not include Headquarters' offices, a large 70-foot drill tower and yard to match. It had been open a couple of years, being one of the busiest stations in the country. Three calls were received whilst we had our stand-easy that morning. None of them required the turntable ladder's attendance that I was driving until after lunch, when we were called to Bow Road with all three appliances. We moved out and turned into Upper North Street. I followed behind the pump escape and pump. My first shout driving the turntable ladder was to prove a disaster. I caught the front wing of a car as I negotiated the tight bends of Upper North Street, a large winding road that certainly wasn't built to accommodate the large 100-foot monster I was driving. No serious damage though, the accident reports kept me busy for the rest of the day. This was my first and only vehicle accident as a Brigade driver, thank heavens. This was a young watch, apart from the Officers and Hooky Walker, an ex-Chinditz soldier and turntable ladder driver. Apart from Hooky, I was senior hand with only six years in.

Station Officer Snelling approached me after only a few days. He asked if I would be willing to act-up to the rank of Leading Fireman. He had a couple of other men on the promotion trail; they were however performing higher duties at other stations. So it was down to me. I had some qualifications and no experience, agreeing to assist in the office with some apprehension. I then spent most of my time assisting other officers with reports, etc. Station Officer Snelling let us get on with it until he signed the completed document, which many times we had to do again and again as they were incorrect. A vast variety of incidents came up at Poplar, many thought of it as a rubbish station. True, however we had as many good 'jobs' comparable with other busy stations. The governor wasn't by any means a strict disciplinarian. He ruled with a magic wand rather than an iron rod, having lost his men at Dudgeon's Wharf. Everything else must have seemed unimportant to him at times. He really was surprisingly laid back at all times. He never mentioned Dudgeon's during my time with him. The watch usually had quite a strict Sub Officer, and he would be allowed to run the watch day to day. The Divisional Staff Office was where the availability of men and appliances was monitored on a daily basis. Staff Officers rode a small control unit and attended larger fires or special service calls.

Called to a man trapped on a building site one day, we arrived with Headquarters' Control Unit. Our arrival saw an upturned dumper truck being removed from a water-filled pit using a crane. The driver had been pinned underneath and wasn't to be seen. We searched the deep pit and on finding him he was resuscitated and removed to hospital, where unfortunately he succumbed to his injuries a month or so later. Our bulk of fires were indeed rubbish or derelict buildings. The London Docks had little shipping passing through them. They stood mainly unused. When a ship fire did occur, they were quite a problem as far as fire-fighting was concerned, due to their size and cargoes. I had attended only a handful of these types of fires and the Brigade had recently lost a fireman from F28 on a ship fire, when he became lost and died in the cargo hold. Another on our watch was killed in a road traffic accident whilst off duty. He was in his early twenties. Station Officer Snelling, Hooky Walker and I, cleared his locker following his death. The Station Officer of course had done this before.

Poplar was busy 24 hours a day. Some jobs came to us. One evening, an old man was mown down by a hit-and-run driver. We attended to this immediately calling an ambulance. He was in such a mess, having severe head injuries. He died in the ambulance as it left the station. During rare periods of inactivity, we would let our hair down and have a water fight or make other mischief. Many 'junior bucks' were sent up the drill tower with a lamp to watch for low-flying aircrafts; this was a common jape, it strangely always worked.

The worst scenario, I felt, was searching for those lost or trapped in fires, if on locating them, they were children, and the fire proved fatal. We had many close calls. I recall Tony Moon and myself searching a Chinese Restaurant in Limehouse. We entered in with breathing apparatus and began to search the accommodation above the premises, both receiving electric shocks, as we touched the stair rail to the first floor. The electric wiring had melted, leaving bare live wires. After our initial shock, we said nothing and allowed one or two senior officers to sample the same, much to our crew's delight. This same incident proved near fatal to us both. As we got to the top floor an extremely large coping stone fell between us, we were lucky that night. Near misses were often encountered, but were part of the job it seemed.

Some of my time was spent in Headquarters Staff, driving the Control Unit or one of the divisional vans (buggies), this made the occasional welcome break from the humdrum of the station, being a lot quieter. The watch were quite socially-minded and arranged many do's, extremely large retirement parties were held in station appliance rooms. This had become a norm for retiring firemen during that period; being involved with these was hard work, but well worth it on the night.

March 1973, I had passed my Leading Fireman's Examinations, and awaited my interview, although on this occasion I was not successful due to general inexperience in the duties of an officer. I remained at F22, but my acting-up duties would now increase at other stations. When this happened, I felt our two dear lady cooks were glad to see the back of me. Especially Ivy, who on one evening whilst she was attempting to prepare our supper, we put into a large dustbin. She couldn't get out as the dustbin was heavy, being storage for our stock of potatoes. We left her to it, intending to release her after a few minutes, but unfortunately we were called out – all of us. On our return an hour later, we found her still in the bin in a foul mood as you can imagine, wish I had a camera. The cooks on all stations, bless them, were indeed the butt of many jokes. I don't know how they put up with it, although they were always remembered on birthdays or at Christmas. Perhaps that made up for it. They seemed to love us one and all.

The job was changing. The Health and Safety at Work Act was in its infancy. The Fire Brigade's Union was well aware of its implications as were the Brigade Authorities.

Appliances, once 'on the run' for many years were being replaced seemingly every two years for more modern efficient vehicles. Even talk of changing the fire gear. Well, it had not changed much in 100 years, although brass helmets had disappeared around 30 years previously, mainly because of the introduction of electricity and the danger of electrocution whilst fire-fighting in those days. Our appliances were changed during the 1970s and beyond, every two or three years. The very old machines would end up in various countries around the world. For me, I had completed and qualified in an emergency tender course. I now had all the practical qualifications you could obtain at that time.

August 1974 saw me promoted and posted to C26 Barbican white watch. I considered refusing the promotion as I loved the F division, however, D.O. John Higginbotham who promoted me, promised I would be back to F division in six weeks. I did go, and had six enjoyable weeks at this station. I was involved in three jobs with the turntable ladders, a few lift incidents and rubbish fires. Yes, I did enjoy Barbican. Fred Hooker was my Station Officer, a real city gent. It was Fred's station who was first on the scene at Moorgate. On my return back to the F division, I was posted to F23 Millwall White Watch, although they saw little of me as I was acting-up or temporarily promoted most of the time, Sub Officer at Poplar, Staff, Homerton, Bethnal Green.

It had taken a while, and I was now enjoying my promotion. I had gained confidence and respect. December 1974 came and Divisional Officer Higginbotham phoned and offered me long-term promotion at F21 Stratford Blue Watch. This was a plum job in a plum station no doubt. The Red Watch here had a reputation that went before them. I accepted and joined the Blue Watch as Sub Officer in January 1975. My aim was to get the job permanently, and after a couple of months I got it, and after such a short time as an Officer, I really was thrown in at the deep end.

Chapter Six

Crème-de-la-crème

Dedicated to the Memory of Station Officer M. Walker.

The Blue Watch F21 would turn out to be the finest I had served on, and I feel they surpassed the Red Watch F21 who had a superb reputation at this time, led by Station Officer Crawley, Sub Officer Walker and Leading Fireman Clarke. Each, in himself, a character, all were fine fire Officers. My governor, Tom Edwins, was frowned upon by many of his peers, although I found him on the fire ground where it matters, quite capable. Ian Powell was the Leading Fireman. As for myself, I needed to gain experience in the running of a station. The Station Officer allowed me to do this. I liked to get 'stuck in' on jobs, and I felt this led the way to my gaining respect from the watch. I was still very much a fireman at heart and at times regretted gaining promotion, although I lost no friends. Eastern Command Control Staff were in the grounds of the station, so if any large incidents were going on, it was interesting to see them at work. These operators shared our mess facilities, so we knew them well. One day in particular, we'd heard of a tube train crash. We'd just come on duty at 0900 hours; our first day. I took our 'junior buck' Dave over to the Control Room. Seeing this was a major incident in progress, we left them to it as it was far too busy in there for them to attend to us... Details to follow on that one.

One occasion all the lads will remember was Fireshow '76, held at Crystal Palace. The summer of '76 broke all records, it was so hot. Luckily for us, we had rigged up a ducking stool over a large water-filled dam. A ball was thrown through a hole and the mechanism dropped the stool into the dam, and damn it was as the stool broke on the first day. However, we hit on the idea of calling 'chuck 'em in for 10p'. Gordon Honeycomb, the then newsreader went in, amongst many others. Jimmy Saville had opened the event and the first day was free for disabled children. I believe we donated part of our takings to the Fire Service Benevolent Fund too. It was over a long weekend, Friday to Monday and we fried. We did however gain around £500 to £600 altogether from our stall. One other collected more, so we had taken the second largest amount over the weekend. We finished up on the Sunday night and on Monday morning we cleared up. The roads were busy and hot as we drove back to Stratford, but we were quite proud of our achievements.

Stratford was an extremely busy station to serve at, not too many rubbish fires like Poplar. We had many house fires due to the nature of the community, and the standard of housing including many rented apartments, flats etc. My first tour of duty went well. I met many of the watch who knew me as a fireman at F22 Poplar. My reputation was one of a bit of a joker, mad even, however, in the main the job came first. Training, teamwork and of course the fire-ground, was where I was to see bravery and gallantry unsurpassed. I had already served with men who had gallantry awards, and I held the utmost respect for them, although perhaps at times it didn't show, ' bit of a rebel too you see'.

Fred Smith, Jimmy Lambeth, George Potts at F27 Bow, Jim Docherty BEM and the whole Red Watch at F29 Leyton all held Chief Officer's commendations. As was Station Officer Harold Snelling at F22 Poplar, for his actions at Dudgeon's Wharf. Finally, Station Officer Mick Walker, deceased, part of the Red Watch F21 Stratford – the total fire-fighter. A chapter would not be enough for all of them, so I will leave it at that.

This watch, the Blue at F21 turned out to be a watch of real fire-fighters, pump operators, ladder-men; they could do it all to a man. The watch at F21 Stratford, Station Officer Griffin, Sub Officer Brian Gurney, Kenny Pauls, Terry Hill, Mick Stothard, Jim Clarke, Steve Lender, Ian Isaac, Dave Hose, John Deans, Dave Easie, Ted Blyth, Dave Handy, Bob Blanch, and Terry Mates. Unfortunately, time dims my memory, perhaps others will crop up later. Ian Powell, my Leading Fireman and right hand man, he too was exceptional and helped me a lot during my early days as a temporary Sub Officer, second officer in charge of perhaps the finest fire-fighting station in the country. I must say that in the eight years I was there, we lost but two lives, both as I remember due to train accidents, not fires. We saved many in my days there. I had not one fatal fire in all my time at F21 Stratford – correct me if I'm wrong lads. I had reached the pinnacle of my career here. Yes, we had our quiet spells, but when busy we were unsurpassed in our own way thanks to the training and at times gallantry; a true dream team. Some shifts we never stopped, in-and-out day-and-night, other times we went for a month maybe with very little to write home about. Many house fires, the pure essence of fire-fighting, were dealt with from this station. Snatch rescues, pet rescues, men, women and children, we had the lot, with more to come in my eight years here at F21.

The first in detail was a rescue of two children and a woman from the first floor of a house in Forest Gate. The smoke so thick I don't know how we found these people, all overcome in a first floor bedroom, even the budgie was saved. Many road traffic accidents. The grandad, out for a day with his grandchildren, who following a low speed accident was to succumb to his injuries days later; the lady who was cut from the car still in her seat following an accident and was taken to hospital with suspected broken neck and back; the drunk who was decapitated under the back of a lorry, all these and more had to be dealt with.

We were called to a child under a bus at Tramway, off Romford Road one evening, and our arrival saw a near 20 foot trail of blood and skid marks from the tyres of the bus. The bus had to be raised by jacks to remove the body. Those were the worst jobs, those involving children. Usually on the return to the station, the men would be involved in some sort of merriment, to get it out of their minds as there was no counselling in those days. It was a weakness and unheard of anyway.

Animals too, had benefited from our fire-fighting skills. The complete evacuation of stables and farm buildings in Leytonstone had been a success. No fatalities, some of the crew received R.S.P.C.A. certificates for their actions that night. I relished this job and felt as one! We had many large fires, ten, fifteen, and twenty- pumpers! They were easy. The small local ones were the best by far. My first four-pumper at Stratford was a fire in a fourth floor flat off High Street, Stratford. No rescues but a good job all round; escape ladder pitched to the fourth floor and breathing apparatus used. I got a little pat on the back for that one. My reputation was, I felt, one of firm but fair, with a little bit of fun included. I hope that sums me up as an Officer. Give and take was my motto, and I felt they all realised that. In fact I know they did. We did drills one evening soon after my arrival at Stratford as things weren't coming together on the fire ground. We had several new recruits and a few Fire Brigade Union motivated individuals. I drilled them till ten minutes to eight o'clock, when I ordered a hook ladder drill. It went ok until an individual, a probationary recruit fireman refused. I ordered him to change into his undress uniform as I was going to charge him for his refusal. I asked Ian Powell to inform Headquarters and ask for an Assistant Divisional Officer to attend.

Meanwhile, Ken came up to me, a fireman I had the utmost respect for and asked if he could talk to the fireman involved. I held fire and waited. He came back out into the drill yard, apologised - then we both did the hook ladder drill together. We shook hands and went to supper at 20:00 hours. That man, Steve Lender, proved to me he was one of the finest firemen I had the pleasure to serve with. Senior Officers too in the F. Division seemed part of the family, if not, they left very soon. Bert Gillings, our Divisional Officer saw to that. He created the family atmosphere within the division, and I have a tie to prove it, compliments of Bert of course. He had many made for members of the division; no one had done that before!

I come now to the Moorgate train disaster. As you read earlier, I was witnessing the start of the operation with our new recruit Dave. The disaster happened at 0900 hours (8.37am to be precise) and was to prove to be one of the most complex jobs ever to be attended by the emergency services. An underground train driven by Mr. Leslie Newton should have been braking. It sped past platform 9 at twice the usual speed of 15 miles per hour, and ran out of track. The first three of six coaches telescoped at the end of the 80 foot tunnel after crashing through sand piles and over buffers. The carriages were over and under each other, had concertinaed and the carriage sides had split within the tunnel. Many of the dead had been found beneath the first carriage. The first fifteen feet had been compacted down to two feet, and embedded into the end wall.

The first day saw doctors, firemen, and nurses

wrestling with the wreckage, in dust and heat, attempting to reach those alive. A trapped teenage policewoman was carried out after twelve hours. One of her feet had been pinned down by the tangle of metal, and had to be amputated at the scene. One young doctor at the scene said "If there is a hell, I've seen it". F21 attended on the first and third days. On the first day, Leading Fireman Powell was in charge and ordered F21's pump to stand by at Moorgate, whilst the cutting away of the first carriage took place from the floor beneath. F27 Bow's crew were involved I believe, Leading Fireman George Sheppard in charge. They cut away the floor to reveal what can only be described to resemble a can of pilchards. The floor removed, George was the first to enter the first badly damaged carriage. It was carnage. Others followed to reveal the hell of the first carriage. Thirty-five people died in there. The roof of the first carriage was on the tunnel roof and two feet below it was the floor. The bogie wheels of the train were overhead, as we found out on the third night when I was in charge of F21 pump. We were involved in the cutting away and removal of carriage metal by oxy-actelyne torches. God it was hot, masks were worn by all, as the smell was indescribable, due to the remaining bodies being trapped for some forty odd hours. We worked whilst about ten bodies remained trapped, including Leslie Newton who was encapsulated in an area of about one foot. Behind was a woman trapped in much the same way. We saw this as, when relieved, my crew members (a young lot) wished to see the first carriage and the bodies. We were allowed to and to be honest, it was unreal, a bit like Madame Tussauds I thought; bodies in tact, as if time had stopped forever. Our time was up and the senior officer on the scene called us out and replaced us with fresh crews. It was eerie down there, cutting noises, then stillness whilst doctors and ambulance crews sounded the carriage. The coffins on the platform, it wasn't Madame Tussauds or a film set, it was for real. We were given washing facilities and the good old Salvation Army offered food from their emergency mobile canteens. We declined, as we had to be decontaminated, which meant a walk through a type of sheep dip and sprays saturating us all over, and asking all of us if we had touched any bodies down there, we hadn't and were allowed to leave for our home station. Some job that.

I wondered what the lads thought. They were quiet on the way home in the back, "serves them right for asking" I thought. The driver was an old hand so he was ok, just another job to him. On our return, everyone was waiting to hear about it. "They'll have to wait till we've cleaned up lads" I said. I doubted we would go down to Moorgate again, we didn't. The bodies including the driver were removed in the early hours of the following day. What a job – terrible. At breakfast the lads joked about the job as they do, self counselling perhaps, except the three who went with me to Moorgate, they declined any breakfast, not that any went to waste though. I think it may have been Dave Handley who polished off the unwanted breakfasts. As with all stations, certainly busy ones, a lot of japes are apparent; like the night Terry Pates went to bed early and we wheeled a motorbike into the dormitory, bump started it, headlights full on towards Terry's bed. He sat up screaming blue murder. As Leading Fireman, I could run with the hare and the hounds. Our new Sub Officer, B. Gurney wore 'clicky' shoes and would click around looking for me or the men; we could easily avoid Brian because of the noise from his shoes. He told me later he had them fitted, so as not to catch anyone out.

In the Fire Service, we use the phonetic alphabet, alpha, bravo, charlie, etc. We had a large chemical fire at Steetley Chemicals one afternoon. The chemical involved was Napthien. The Officer in Charge sent back his message via the driver, fireman Handley, who to everyone's delight except the Divisional Commander, sent a lovely message back to control. He said "n – Norman, a – Alice, p- Peter, t – Tom," etc. The Commander went mad, but the lads did such a good job, we felt he let us off. Another time, Fireman Dewie was asleep in the dormitory. A couple of us crept in and gave him a beard and moustache in black felt tip pen. He didn't notice it until the morning when we had an early call to Stratford Centre.

Chapter Seven

Boys from 21

This watch was special for me. A new Station Officer arrived, Station Officer Terry Griffin. We worked well together, and when Brian Gurney joined us the watch was in the main, complete. We were busy, not just fires, the Romford Road supplied us with many road traffic accidents and special services, i.e. lift jobs, etc. We'd had many jobs, the funniest seemed to be with animals with many a canine having been rescued and put in a place of safety. They would then proceed to bite their rescuers. The kitten that got blasted by a gas jet and lived to tell the tale, horses, dogs, and cats in canals, kestrels up trees, they flew away too. I was annoyed as I was perched 85 foot up on a turntable ladder to rescue them.

We arrived at a fire in a pet shop. On forcing entry we saw many snakes and reptiles on the floor. As we entered further, one lad in breathing apparatus gave a muffled cry. He had been grabbed around the neck by a chimpanzee. Many pets escaped, never to be seen again. Pets formed part of the stations in the 1800s; dogs ran along with the fast moving horse-drawn steamer fire-engine. Cats too, they adopted a rather more leisurely life style waiting for the men to return.

Today you may find a thriving tropical fish tank in some stations. Unlike budgies and canaries, dogs and cats rescued from smoky conditions soon came round, some didn't. I was on duty at F29 Leyton one day, all very quiet until 3.30p.m. We were called to a house fire at Palmerston Road. Turning at the top of the road, we saw a ball of black smoke. Two window cleaners stood at the door, telling us nobody was in the house. I "made pumps four" as the crew gained entry through upper windows. Half an hour later saw the fire extinguished, not unfortunately, without loss. A large black Labrador was found nearby to the seat of the fire. The next door neighbour told us to put the dog over the fence, and he would bury it. There was in fact, a person in the house; the owner. He jumped from a first floor rear window, and he was uninjured. The cause of the fire was a domestic gas pipe becoming disengaged from the meter.

One job that does stick in my mind is one time when both appliances were called to a house fire. Station Officer Griffin on the pump, myself on the pump Escape. We arrived and tackled a fire in a lean-to greenhouse. The fire extinguished, we went to the front of the house where about six bird cages were lined up, and a middle aged lady sobbing on the doorstep. I stood for a few minutes when the Station Officer came up to me and in an angry tone said "I think you can sod off now Terry". My thoughts were, 'what have I done wrong?' Still puzzled, we returned to the station and restocked the used hose. Station Officer Griffin appeared ten minutes later, grinning all over his face. What's up with him, I thought, had the hump ten minutes ago. "Oi Terry, come here" he called. I approached him and he continued. "Sorry I sent you off with a flea in your ear, but I thought you'd dropped one, only to find out that the lady who was crying so much had shit herself," a common occurrence in shock. Griff – Station Officer Griffin – was a fine man and an excellent Governor. One of the best I felt, on the fire ground and on the station. He was also very good in assisting junior officers. Terry is a lifelong friend.

Early morning calls were always attended with tongue in cheek. A cigarette shop in Stratford High Street was well alight when we smashed the plate glass window and entered, Mick Stothard and myself. We knew children were reported upstairs. As we reached the stairs, Mick and I left the branch and got out quickly. As we reached the doorway, a flashover occurred. Something must have warned us of that, a sixth sense maybe. In a flashover, nothing survives. We re-entered, and with crews fighting the blaze, went upstairs to search the upper floors. All rooms searched, and no children were found. The police were in attendance to secure the burned out premises, and we left thinking no more about it.

Coming on duty one spring evening, we heard talk of the White Watch called to a 30-stone man who required lifting to his chair, which they did. A call at 22:00 hours was to the same man. On arrival, we saw the gentleman on the floor; he was enormous. He had a false leg; his other leg was sore and red, with the skin peeling. It was gangrenous. We tried for an hour, lifting him with lengths of flat hose to no avail. He was in pain and the hose was cutting into him. After a further hour, he asked us to leave. He was weak and tired. He couldn't help himself at all. He unfortunately died a few days later. I always felt that this was one job at which we failed.

We often played jokes on new recruits. One of the lads would dress up, dog collar and all, as the Brigade Missionary. We did three at Stratford; the recruits concerned had to say prayers. It lasted about an hour, finishing with the whole watch getting together for prayers. We had many pranks played on us, but we also played them on our civilian chef, Edna. We placed a walkie-talkie radio into the plate warmer and out of sight. We had another radio and quietly spoke into it with ghostly tones. Edna didn't show any response, except that she looked around cautiously every time the radio was operated. It was only when we turned it up, that she panicked and ran downstairs. We let her in on the joke moments later. Jim Clarke got a clip round the ear hole from the cook, and I got a telling off by the Governor.

One evening, we made a very large furry rat - tail and all - tied him to a fishing line and placed it outside the fire station, then slowly drew him in for all to see. Some people hit the rat, some screamed, and some ran. I can assure you, it was so funny to see. We were all in tears of laughter. A couple with dogs passed by, the dogs never bothered, perhaps it wasn't smelly enough. This jape lasted a few weeks; we then heard other stations were copying our rat race, so we called it a day.

So many calls, too many to remember, came and went. Moorgate and the fireman's strike; two shocking incidents I will never forget. There was another; Cranbrooke Road, Ilford. Stratford's pump was ordered on to a four-pump fire. Station Officer Griffin, Terry Hill driving, Mick Stothard and myself. On arrival, our crew dispersed and the Officer in charge ordered Mick and I to don breathing apparatus. We did not have the new easier-to-use compressed air sets; we were in the changeover period. Mick and I were told to rig and await instructions at the Divisional Control Unit, which we did. Our Station Officer was around the back of the building and Terry Hill at the front. It was a fish and chip shop, with two floors above it. Mick and I were ordered to "start up" and enter at the front on the ground floor. No sooner had we done the start-up, there was an almighty explosion; ladders blown down and across appliances, glass was everywhere. The Officer in charge sent a message to Control; it was "An explosion has occurred, roll calls being taken. Four ambulances required". Mick and I knew roughly where the rest of our crew were, so we booked in on the roll call and proceeded to the back of the building to find our Station Officer. We soon found him; he was assisting a badly injured fireman. "Terry," he screamed, "Take hold of this bloke, I'm injured myself". We carried the chap out. All of the injured – around twenty personnel - were moved to a place of safety on the pavements on the other side of Cranbrooke Road. Ambulances ferried back and forth.

Griff was indeed badly hurt; he had been blown from the third floor. We assisted him as well to the awaiting ambulance. We found Terry Hill outside the shop, with blood all over one hand. I thought he had lost his hand at first, he was lucky, blown through the plate glass when the gas explosion occurred. Both Terry and the Station Officer were removed to hospital with all the others that were injured. I drove the pump back, with Mick Stothard aside of me. It's a strange feeling, when you return to base with two men short. Cannot say this job doesn't have its ups and downs, can we? Many injuries, many minor, occurred in the job, cuts, burns etc.

I remember a particular fire in Forest Gate. On arrival, the first floor was well alight. Myself and another fireman entered in compressed air breathing apparatus to search the upper floors. God, it was so hot. We opened up doors and tried to make the area ventilated. On locating the fire, we asked one of our new recruits to open the door further. He did, and was badly burned on the palm of his hands; the door was glass, we hadn't realised. An ambulance was called, and we put the fire out with a lot of cutting away and damping down to do. As I worked in the street clearing debris, I saw John our newest recruit, sitting in the ambulance with dressing on both hands. As a joke, I said "Come on John, we need help clearing up here". The ambulance man jumped up and explained the degree of his burns to me most irately. I couldn't be bothered to tell him that I was only joking. Funny thing though, John was half out of the ambulance following my 'orders'.

Time went on, the Fire Brigade Authorities and the Union were head to head on our latest pay deal. After many meetings, the Fire Brigade voted for a national strike, much to the surprise of London especially. This strike was to change life in the Fire Brigade forever. Many men said they wouldn't go on strike, but in the main we got a hundred percent from full-time members. This was also to change my life completely; the job was never the same for me again, and many others too. We were a hundred percent behind the Union membership, and many were extremely angry about the way we were being treated. We felt special within society; we are special. Many of my acquaintances and friends would not be on strike, due to belonging to the National Association of Fire Officers. The Senior Officers Union, some were in both, Fire Brigades Union, and National Association of Fire Officers. Some had gone sick, but came on to the picket line. Many booked themselves off sick and joined us 'proper' on the picket line. The public support was a hundred percent behind us. Many calls had been received and we wondered if the Army could cope. They did, as far as they could, bless 'em.

Chapter Eight

Firestrike '78

Many non-strikers reaped the subsequent benefits of the strike of '78. Many of them were crucified, many not spoken to for several months. Day by day, national newspapers were left in our picket huts. The claim following four independent enquiries each, recommending a substantial increase in pay and reduction in hours. Firemen worked a 48-hour week for 20% below the national average wage. During the last year, 342 firemen were seriously injured and 5 killed whilst on duty. 464 people were rescued in London alone. I found that my children could have had free school meals before the strike. We were witnessing the first national firemen's strike. A sad day. A day I will remember forever.

Red Watch had been on duty all night for the strike and picket duty at 9am. I remained in the station until everyone else had departed, and I stepped out of the station last. I needed to do that. Buses, taxis, cars, all stopped to look as we lined up in front of the station, as if to be shot. Many of us were to be, in a way, never to ride to a shout again. Some of the finest went that way, to resign; unable to face the guilt they deeply felt. It was never the same again. A hundred percent; that was the feeling of the membership of full-time fire-fighters, however, some part-timers remained to the dismay of many. Stratford had 2000 plus calls a year.

Merlin Rees, Labour Home Secretary, said "Stand by your buckets". The Prime Minister – Callaghan - would not budge, 10% or nothing. In November 15th 1978, a fire broke out at St. Andrews Hospital in Bow. More than 100 people were evacuated by firemen from nearby Bow Station. Was this the first sign of the strike breaking? It was not. A report came out from the union to reveal the massive support, so far as number 11 region London was concerned. One appliance at G Division was reportedly manned by non-union members. This was not however mobilised by Controls. The National Association of Fire Officers, after voting against the strike, kept their heads down in the main. Some even visited the picket lines with mixed feelings from the strikers, and many stayed at home.

Each watch; Red, White, and Blue formed a duty roster for picket attendance; three members of each watch selected for each duty shift. We remained with our watch members. I recall Jim Clarke and Terry Griffin with me, also fire prevention Station Officer Barry Short, a good friend of mine; that was our crew for picket duty. It was extremely cold, and fires were lit on station forecourts, sheds built, timber supplied by passing lorries, etc, and donations of goods and monies were received. So much so, that the Fire Brigades Union formed a 'fighting fund' and the cash was taken to a selected 'safe house', I suppose you'd call it, to be counted and banked. We received £11 each after the strike; such was the generosity of the public. The Labour Government still would not budge; 10% or nothing was the call. Pay rise percentages were much higher than that of today. Meetings followed meetings to no avail. One call was to resign en bloc.

The press had a field day. Several fatal fires had occurred around the country. The Army fire-fighters did their best. London had its fair share too, large fires occurred including a fatal fire in Leytonstone, the next station to us. Public support remained strong, although the men at Leytonstone had been subjected to cries of 'murderers' by a small number of passers by. This caused many fine firemen never to return to work, feeling they had indeed let the public down. None of us wanted this, but pay was so low, combined with a 48-hour week; it was hard to make ends meet on our money alone. Many worked part-time, and my wife Jeanne and I, were fortunate that she was offered her old secretarial job back. I too had a call from my old part-time boss offering me a job until the strike was over.

They saved the day. Prior to that, I had driven a taxi for a week or so, combined with a little security work on building sites. It was sink or swim; we aimed on a strike lasting days not weeks or months. I spent much of the time collecting daily newspapers left in our 'strike hut', and made up several scrap books of cuttings on the fire strike. Many strikers had jobs; some applied and got DSS benefits for their families. We found our creditors, in the main, most helpful; the Anglia Building Society froze our payments until we resumed work, others did likewise, and it all helped us to fight on.

We dug our heels in feeling more and more bitter as the days went by. Press reporting waned as time passed. We sat and waited, occasionally attending person-reported fires locally. We carried breathing apparatus in one car and four of us would go to the scene. We were never required. Fires had decreased; such was the impact of the strike. People were far more careful; our hopes were raised and darkened many times during the nine weeks of this terrible strike. The Government stood as firm as we did. 10,000 soldiers were on fire-fighting duties by the ninth day. We occasionally saw the soldiers and allowed them on to the stations for showers, after they had attended a blaze or incident. There was no problem between striking firemen and the soldiers.

One document we received at the stations stated 'fire losses for 1976 totalled £231m, fire losses for Wednesday 16th November totalled £200m estimated'. Employer's offers were received on 9th December 1977. This was rejected. On 5th January 1978, the offer was accepted following a recalled Fire Brigade Union Conference at Bridlington. We got a 10% increase and a promise of bringing firemen's wages up to match the manual workers upper-quartile agreements. The voting at the Conference was 28,729 For, to 11,795 Against. The week of the 7th, 8th and 9th of January 1978, London Fire-fighters voted on the latest offer from Employers, and recommendations from the Fire Brigade's Union. They voted NO, but returned to work on 16th January, following a YES vote nationally.

We returned to work on the morning of Monday 16th
January. Morale was at an all-time low nationally.
The Firemen had won, and accepted the initial offer
with much, much more for the future. One quote I
will always remember from those bitterly cold
snowy nights on the picket lines was from Reg
Wilcox, a fine fireman from our watch. He said, 'In a
year or so's time, many of us will have some mental
traumas from all this". His words rang in my ears,
and he was proved to be right; not only did many
fine firemen leave the job, after resuming work it
was to affect me in years to come.

Following weeks saw reprisals and recriminations
to many non-strikers, especially the part-
time/retained firemen of other brigades. Being
forbidden to do so by the Authorities ensured a little
stability, but many suffered at the hands of the
strikers' wrath, our job was never to be the same
again. To bring firemen up to the upper quartile,
pay rises were: 1978/9 - 10%, 1979/80 - 22.5%,
1980/81 - 20.7%, 1981/82 - 10.1%. They also got a
42-hour working week and Red, White and Blue
watches were joined by the newly-formed Green
watch. I managed to stay at F21 Stratford Blue
watch, many had moved here and there following
this new rota system. Our appliances were now
pump escape and pump, and a new addition; a
hose-laying lorry. We were even busier from then
on. We were now back to work. I retained my
temporary Sub officer rank following the strike. We
tried to continue as normal. I had served twelve
years. Little did I know, I had only 7 years left in

this career that I so relished.

One of our first large fires after the strike was a four-pumper in button-makers. I had never seen so many buttons strewn everywhere, such was the state of the place. We had difficulty entering the fire due to millions of very slippery plastic buttons on the floor; it was incredible. The Governor got a bollocking for not making pumps six. We all choked from the acrid fumes of these buttons destroyed in the fire; lungs never to repair. Exactly one year after the strike, we lost Reg Wilcox due to retirement. Reg hadn't quite got his thirty years in, but he was happy to go. We had a retirement do for him and managed to find him a fireman's brass helmet. His retirement do was on the 4th November at L's 'A' Poppin at East Ham. Jeanne and I left around 10pm, as she was expecting and the baby was overdue. We drove to Harold Wood Hospital, with Jim and Bobby Clarke in tow. Our second son Steven was born at 1am on 5th November 1979. He would be our third child, keeping Julie and Kevin company.

The formation of the further watch, the Green Watch, was in the early stages. Recruiting was stepped up to enable the new watch to lessen our 48/56-hour duty rota. This change caused much friction; men had to be selected by the Divisional Officer Mr. Bert Gillings. Many men from Red, White and Blue watches were posted on to the new Green watch. He did a wonderful job to ensure that the new watch met the high standards of the other experienced wise officers and men. The new watch system allowed us to do a 2-2-4 day rota: two nine-hour days, two fifteen-hour nights, followed by four days leave, a 48-hour week. Station Officer Barry Short was in charge of Green watch; he'd see them right, a true disciplinarian to say the least, and still a good friend.

In my mind, we had the best watch to this day. We had the finest crew, officers and men that anyone would wish to be associated with, let alone be part of it. I was now reverted to Leading Fireman rank again. I could 'get stuck in' once more, and I did. This watch could fight fires anywhere from forests to factories. We did many rescue jobs and received much accolade. No war-time soldier could have served with the group of men that I had the pleasure to serve with, heroes is a word that gives them little credit. They were magnificent to serve with, one and all. I wished I'd had a camera with me to enlighten you with my words. Oh yes, at times it was an easy job but others not so. We went to situations and places where angels would fear to tread. London's Burning is nothing to what we saw and did, although full credit to the programme.

Chapter Nine

Four Watches

The formation of the four watches; Red, White Blue and Green. The Officers and men had been selected, albeit one or two dissenters; green watch would go ahead. We lost Kenny Pauls to green watch here at Stratford, and Sub Officer Brian Gurney to green watch F29 Leyton as Station Officer in charge. I acted-up once again under Station Officer Griffin. We had now gained a further appliance, a hose-laying lorry, and also two Leading Firemen instead of one, Jim Clarke and John Hood covering those two ranks. We carried on as before, going further afield with the hose-laying lorry. The Ford Motor Company at Dagenham was one run we did. The station was busier than ever – great. The first few weeks were taken up with getting to know the workings of the hose-laying lorry. We un-stowed and re-stowed the lorry many times. We also trained with the heavy-lifting gear that this vehicle carried. We missed the two men we had lost to Green Watch, although Ken Pauls did return to us at a later date. We had a meal at a restaurant to say farewell to the lads who went to Green Watch; they would be sorely missed. More had left the job after the strike. None of Blue Watch left so we were lucky, much the same watch as before the changeover. One or two new recruits, Andy McGelligan and John Lowe, joined us. They were soon knocked into shape and enjoyed working with the watch.

We were called to a car fire at Union Street in March 1980; both appliances from F21 attended, plus F27 Bow's pump. On arrival, myself and Mick Stothard located a man slumped over the wheel of his smoke-filled car. We pulled him out, but he was apparently dead. As soon as he hit the floor, Mick and I were working on him; Mick giving cardiac massage and I giving him mouth-to-mouth. The man came round on two occasions and then lapsed. We kept trying and he became conscious and walked to the ambulance totally unaware of what had happened. On our return to the station, we were confronted with two Senior Officers awaiting full details of the incident and any recommendations to the Commander. In 1982, both Mick Stothard and myself received the Royal Humane Resuscitation Certificate for restoring this man to life. Mick now has two certificates, one from an earlier incident. He is possibly the only person to hold two of these awards. He also gained the British Empire Medal for services to the Brigade. We had to attend a big ceremony for us both to be presented with our awards. We were last on the presentation list and it seemed hours, finding out later the higher the award, the later the presentation. These ceremonies were held between a year and eighteen months apart, and both of us felt very proud to receive this honour.

It was soon after the incident with the man in the car, that we had a fatal incident involving a railway carriage at Stratford Station. I didn't attend, being on the hose-laying lorry and not required. The guys came back, and you could see by their faces it was grim working under that train for an hour or so. This was my last call at F21. I was posted to Red watch F23 Millwall in 1982 under Station Officer Alan Chart, who had previously been the Governor at F21 Stratford Blue Watch since Station Officer Griffin retired in 1981. On my leaving Stratford, the watch had a little 'do' for me. A pewter mug was presented. However, it was sad to leave F21 Stratford, but I had had enough of busy stations. I had been in 16 years with mortgage, wife and three children; small wonder I was knackered. I arrived at Millwall with my gear and the watch helped me with it to the Leading Fireman's locker room. F23 was an old station, a 1910 building much in the same mould as Bow. The watch was a good one, although things got done at a more leisurely pace here. No sooner had I placed my fire gear on the appliance, we had a call to some cars alight in garages.

The truth in my going to Red Watch F23, was so I would stand a better chance of getting the job at F Divisional Headquarters Staff as one of the two Sub Officers. Ron Randall was the other Sub Officer at that time, and I loved working with Ron. I did get to Staff Headquarters, but not in the way I expected. Having only been at F23 a matter of weeks, I injured my back, neck and shoulder at an incident. I was off duty for a month, returning on light duty day work at Divisional Headquarters Staff Poplar. I was checking the mail and fire reports, it couldn't have been more boring. Joe Kennedy was now in charge of the Division; a real gentleman. After every job we had, he would be out of his office to see all was well and to be told about the incident. We had some fine Senior Officers; even Brian Robinson, now Chief of London Fire Brigade; Harry White, my colleague in Health and Safety; Mick Edwards, the joker; Sub Officer Arthur Davies as Staff Station Officer, and good friend.

Ron and I ran the Red Watch office very well, although I wasn't quite the fire-fighter I had been. I felt a lack of concentration, being in the service 17 years and only 37. I visited my doctor and he prescribed minor tranquilisers. Ron knew I was struggling at the time, hopefully not affecting our work, that's what friends are for, although I didn't take liberties and always rode the Divisional Control Unit. Les Goldsmith was our Assistant Divisional Officer. We seemed to have moved around the Division together. Joe Kennedy had been in London as a Station Officer. He then transferred to Essex, now returning as Assistant Chief Officer. A nicer chap you couldn't wish to meet, an excellent Fire Officer, very pro-Fire Brigade and Fire Services Benevolent Fund.

Whilst on light duty, I attended a 10-week Health and Safety at Work Course, which I passed and became Health and Safety Rep for the Fire Brigade's Union in F Division. On being placed back on full duty, I remained at 'F' Divisional Headquarters as temporary Sub Officer with Ron Randall, which suited me fine at the time. Much of my off duty hours were spent doing inspections on fire stations and drill locations. Divisional Officer Harry Evans was Brigade Health and Safety

Officer, and we worked well together. So well in fact, that one day Joe Kennedy was heard to retort "Don't you ever get any aggro here?" He loved a little aggro, did Joe. We inspected all the stations and reported on Health and Safety issues or complaints. My main duties lay with Ron in the Staff Office. We rode the Divisional Control Unit to major fires or incidents. I saw more dead bodies in my time at Headquarters than at any time in my career. This affected me, I wasn't coping as I should, and my bottle was going. I had heard that said about others before now, although I carried on regardless as we had so many large interesting fires and incidents. My injuries were worsening, seeing the Medical Officer on several occasions, remaining on full duty following each medical. I was enjoying Staff work; getting the availability of men and machines at each of the F Divisions nine stations, covering stand-bys for those stations when short with annual and public holiday leave, and numerous other tasks in the office. When Ron was on leave, we usually had another Sub Officer in to cover, as two men were required to man the unit. Sometimes Leading Firemen took the roll, so I got to know an awful lot of guys as they came up to Headquarters on temporary promotion, awaiting interviews, etc.

The Divisional Control Unit was busy. A large fire and explosion on Millwall's ground occurred one evening. Sid Brand, my driver, was rather panicky with all the goings-on. I suddenly realised Sid was a survivor of the Dudgeon's Wharf fire many years previous. He served at Millwall at the time, and this incident wasn't a stone's throw from the Wharf that had blown many of his colleagues to their deaths. I kept Sid out of the way at this incident. It must have brought it all back to him. It didn't do me much good, as on arrival a large gas cylinder blew up flying metal everywhere, but luckily no-one was hurt.

On another occasion, we went on relief to a fatal fire in Brick Lane. They were still in the building but I had no wish to see them, also hoping I would not be asked to move them. A year or so ago it wouldn't have bothered me, but now it made me shiver; having been to many fatal fires and never being too bothered about them, even the Moorgate Train crash. I wasn't coping at all well, and I told Ron of my feelings. He seemed to think it happened to a lot of fire fighters at some stage. "Don't worry about it" he said. Ron realised it had affected me as it does to this day. I was always working, fire-fighting, or working at home at this pace. I feel that's what caused my illness, rather than the job. I loved it, and the guys and girls in it. I knew nearly everyone on the Red and Blue watches due to my Staff work and many from the other two watches.

It was a great atmosphere at Staff. I also knew all the Senior Officers due to my work at Headquarters and my Health and Safety at Work duties. Joe Kennedy was my Commander for some time. He would often oversee the Health and Safety work, with interest; he never interfered. Ron and I had worked so long together, we were almost telepathic. To this day, Ron is still a good friend along with many more. I had so much to thank Albert Smith for, a job for life and a pension.

Chapter 10

Grounded

My trips to the Medical Officer for my back problem were regular. I was however, passed fit for duty every time. I never mentioned my anxieties. Meanwhile, Ron and I were working hard. It was a busy Division. We had attended chemical or oil spillages, four to ten-pump fires, incidents in the docks, persons trapped in machinery, etc. We were a good team; and with Les Goldsmith, Sid, Albert and Barry, we were a happy bunch too, like family really. Ron knew all mine, and he taught my wife Jeanne to drive. He saw Julie, Kevin and Steven grow up. We've had many nicknames in the fire service, but not everybody gets one. I believe mine at Stratford was BASTARD. Ron Randall's was ROSY, to name but two.

Most nights we had a couple of fire calls between us, and perhaps the van had to pick up some hose or equipment from fires and incidents. We saw a lot of the lads from the station; sometimes they drove one of our vehicles. Station Officer Tom Westerham was the Red Watch Governor. It was important to work well with them too, they were a tough watch at Poplar Red Watch; they loved a laugh and were excellent firemen to a man. One of my main involvements whilst in Staff Headquarters was with Health and Safety at Work, and I worked for the Fire Brigades Union alongside deputy assistant Chief Officer Kennedy and Divisional Officer Evans. I, along with a Senior Officer, would inspect stations regularly and be in attendance at combined drills. Stations were also checked from the appliance pit to the water tanks in the attic. Health and Safety was going to be big. Much work was done following our inspection. The Union was apparently equipped more so than the Brigade with Health and Safety at this time (early '80's). We had meetings between Union and Management once a fortnight. Health and Safety covered everything: hazards, near-miss accidents, accidents to personnel and equipment, and so much more. Remember, I was in on the early days, as far as the London Fire Brigade was concerned, and at times it was hit and miss initially.

I was finding the job heavy-going now. I injured my shoulder again. I was worried about seeing the Medical Officer. Needless to say, something happened to change all that. I was off duty on the night in question; Ron Randall was on duty and in attendance at a fire. Ron, being Ron, was assisting the men when the floor collapsed under him injuring his legs and hips, causing him to be off work for a considerable time. Ron came back to work, but he was in pain. All those years ago in 1967, I was on my first fire call with Ron, and now on my last call Ron was there too. We were called to a 'four-pump persons reported' on Bethnal Green's ground. We arrived to find the crews searching for a baby who had been left on its own. The baby was found in a baby bouncer, burned through, with its arms and legs gone too. It looked like a chicken.

After our duty was done, I said to Ron "Sod this,

I've had enough", and Ron agreed it was a very nasty job. Ron went sick with his injuries again only weeks later. I was now in Staff as Watch Sub Officer. I really couldn't cope with this job at all. I anxiously asked Divisional Officer Parker, whom I had known since 1967, if I could come off operational duties and do training or fire prevention, both day duties. I felt I couldn't stay operationally employed.

Within a week I was moved to the Fire Prevention Branch in Stratford as Sub Officer, with Divisional Officer Smythe, Divisional Officer Taylor, Station Officer Brittle, Station
Officer Smith, along with many others. I was employed alongside Sub Officer Norman. We did school lectures all over the East End. I could have had the job permanently, but for my back and shoulder trouble. I was still under the Medical Officer. I did Fire Prevention inspections, sometimes on my own, but more often than not with John Brittle and Brian Smith. They knew the job like the back of their hand. I still missed Station life and watched the lads go out on fire calls at Stratford, as our offices were above the station. I spent several months in Fire Prevention and I enjoyed serving under Divisional Officer John Taylor, a true hardworking gentleman.

One day, I was called up for what was to be my final medical. I was claimed 'P.U'd' (permanently unfit). It was February 1985; I had served nineteen years. I felt relief and sadness all at once. In my final weeks, Ron Randall who like me was also on light duty, came to Fire Prevention Branch and we worked together doing the vast amount of filing that was required in that department. If I hadn't had enough by now, I did after doing this, anyway! Ron retired a few months later. For me, Brian Smith and Mick Page, whom I had known all the time in my career, arranged a retirement do. I carried on with my work in Fire Prevention Branch. I had no idea, and was very anxious on leaving. I was married, with three children and a mortgage to boot. My pension would barely touch that. My retirement do was held at Stubbs Club a few doors up from Stratford Fire Station, and next to the swimming pool in Romford Road. People came from every station; Control Room staff and Fire Prevention Branch. Mr. Bert Gillings gave his usual first class speech, and I received so many gifts from Stations that I hadn't even served on. A grand evening was held for me and I am proud of the lot of you. Thank you.

Soon after, Red Watch Stratford invited Jeanne and I to a retirement do. It was Alfie Jones' time to go. We went and I was presented with a bronze statuette and Jeanne received flowers. I don't remember much of either of these do's, although the mornings after I remember sitting amongst all my gifts, crying my eyes out.

With my uniform etc. handed in and my pension set up, I felt I was alone in a big wide world. It was March 1985. I was 38 years old and a near-broken man. What job could I do with these injuries? The worry made me even more anxious. However, I did get a job as a carer for two weeks, but their Medical Officer soon stopped that. We managed on pension and the dole. Perhaps, I would write a book about those I had served with, some of the finest of course. Regrets, yes, very much so on leaving, but I could see myself going. The traumas in my mind were more apparent and my back, neck and sides were causing lots of problems. I was half the man I was, or should have been. I had worked with some of the finest, too many to be named within these pages. I apologise for that. Perhaps, had I gone for further promotion to Divisional Officer even, my health may not have suffered? I was so interested in do-it-yourself work or part-time work, that I had neglected my career as far as promotion was concerned. Divisional Officer John Higginbotham said on promoting me, "I want to see you a Station Officer by the time I retire". Unhappily, I only made it to Sub-Officer. It's only when you leave and meet people from different walks of life, that it really shows how much respect the fire-fighters have; that kept me going, also keeping in touch with Mick Stothard, Jim Clarke, etc.

I felt I was a failure and was often found reading my citation from the Royal Humane Society following a rescue of a man in 1980. I, of course, wasn't a failure.

Chapter Eleven

Fire of Doves

Dedicated to the Memory of G. Haughey

From boy to man, I'd been a fireman; serving with some of the finest one could wish to meet, but what for me now? Tried several jobs, couldn't manage. Not much work around for an injured, retired fireman. After a year, I felt maybe I could do my own business; carpet and upholstery cleaning struck me. I bought the machinery and did a training course. On my own, I struggled for about six years. Believe me, the Fire Service was easier than this. I kept going until my eldest son was 18. I then gave the business to him and his younger brother. I worked at a small, local engineering firm as a cleaner, van driver and a little fireman-ship. Whilst working there, I had a call from the Chief Fire Officer of News International; his name was George Baker. Along with John Brittle and Mick Page, both ex-London Firemen, we joined the Fire Department at Wapping, home of *The Sun* and *The Times Daily Newspapers*. One of our duties was to ensure that no one smoked in the plant and to check all the fire-fighting installations and equipment regularly, on top of fire-fighting duties. We had a few incidents, spillages, small fires, but nothing substantial.

My anxiety states were worsening and I was having difficulty coping with this relatively easy job. Doctors offered me tranquilisers, antidepressants, etc. etc. This forced me to leave News International after a year, which I had in the main, enjoyed. I thought I'd continue carpet cleaning, as the boys didn't seem bothered. That's all I had. Within a fortnight of leaving News International, I was taken by ambulance to hospital with a severe nervous breakdown. Five times I was to go that way. A community psychiatric nurse, Mr. Don Karandasa, came to see me and recommended I go to Basildon Mind. I did, and remained doing counselling work for ten years under Mrs. Sheila Chesney. This place and the staff and volunteers saved me, without them I would have possibly taken my own life.

I was asked to serve on the Executive Committee and act as Fire Officer for the organisation, which I did. Three years later, saw me as Vice Chairman of the Executive Committee of Basildon Association of Mental Health, Basildon Mind. I saw the organisation build up from one small drop-in centre with four staff; to one Head Office with four staff, one counselling centre with four staff and twenty volunteer counsellors, one-drop in centre with fifteen staff caring for one hundred members, and finally five group homes run by Mrs. Dot Pike. Hopefully, we may be able to get funded for our own charity shop and eventually a halfway-house sanctuary for those suffering the traumas of mental illness, but not ill enough for our overworked and over-crowded hospitals.

The End - the end of the line for me perhaps, but not for our boss Mrs. Sheila A Chesney, she'll never stop. Her objectives are clear. A new drop-in centre, a shop, and a safe house were her goals. She has her new drop-in centre, and the shop and safe house are next. I am at this moment unable to assist, as my health changes so quickly. It will be interesting to watch, being still involved as a volunteer, until I retire. It's very therapeutic, believe me. Les Goldsmith is Chief Fire Officer for the organisation and last but not least an ex-Romford fireman Laurie Beedon, has worked as a volunteer and a member of staff for the last four years. As you have probably gathered, even though the organisation is so large, it is still like an extension to my family.

Truly. The End.

The Fire-braves, Ultimate Sacrifice

The call sounds for all to hear
All heed and run to help.
Fire, crash, persons trapped, who knows?
They slip into their gear, no fear.
Engines start, on they climb,
Opening doors unleash these braves
They go to a fate unknown.
Explosions heard, they near their goal
A fireball lights the sky
Turning wheels, the scene is seen
Two have jumped, one is trapped
Two braves don breathing sets
Into hell they go to seek
Inferno's child cannot be found
A cry back room is heard by both
They turn and hear a child
Leader in he slips and falls
The raging fire strengthens
From a gap in smoke, a child is plucked
From hell to mother's arms
Alive he is for all to see
Fallen hero still inside
A crew is called and in they go
Too late t'is now explosion two
Rips heart and soul from all
Down to earth this job brings them
Their colleague is no more
50/50 - that's the chance.
The child lived and grew a man.
The brave, he died, an angel now
A guardian for his kind.

A Fireman's Prayer

When I am called to duty God,
Wherever flames may rage,
Give me the strength to save some life
Whatever be its age.

Help me embrace a little child
Before it is too late
Or save an older person from
the horror of that fate.

Enable me to be alert
And hear the weakest shout,
And quickly and efficiently
To put the fire out.

I want to fill my calling, and
To give the best in me
To guard my every neighbour
And protect his property.

And if according to my fate,
I am to lose my life,
Please bless with your protecting hand
My children and my wife.

Amen

Terry Beresford

98

The Firemans Prayer

When I am called to duty God, wherever flames may rage,
Give me the strength to save a life, whatever be its age,
Help me embrace a little child before it is too late,
Or save some older person from the horror of that fate,
Enable me to be alert, and hear the weakest shout,
And quickly and efficiently, to put the fire out,
I want to fill my calling and give the best in me,
To guard my every neighbour, and protect his property,
And if according to your will, I have to lose my life,
Please bless with your protecting hand, my children and my wife.